LEARN MEDIA LITERACY SKILLS

HOW TO DISTINGUISH
FACT FROM OPINION

by Kurt Waldendorf

BrightP◆int Press

San Diego, CA

© 2025 BrightPoint Press
an imprint of ReferencePoint Press, Inc.
Printed in the United States

For more information, contact:
BrightPoint Press
PO Box 27779
San Diego, CA 92198
www.BrightPointPress.com

ALL RIGHTS RESERVED.
No part of this work covered by the copyright hereon may be reproduced or used in any form or by any means—graphic, electronic, or mechanical, including photocopying, recording, taping, web distribution, or information storage retrieval systems—without the written permission of the publisher.

LIBRARY OF CONGRESS CATALOGING-IN-PUBLICATION DATA

Name: Waldendorf, Kurt, author.
Title: How to distinguish fact from opinion / by Kurt Waldendorf.
Description: San Diego, CA: BrightPoint Press, 2025 | Series: Learn media literacy skills |
   Audience: Grade 7 to 9 | Includes bibliographical references and index.
Identifiers: ISBN: 9781678209780 (hardcover) | ISBN: 9781678209797 (eBook)
The complete Library of Congress record is available at www.loc.gov.

CONTENTS

AT A GLANCE	4
INTRODUCTION PODCASTING THE PANDEMIC	6
CHAPTER ONE WHAT ARE FACTS AND OPINIONS?	12
CHAPTER TWO FACTS AND OPINIONS IN TRADITIONAL MEDIA	22
CHAPTER THREE FACTS AND OPINIONS ON THE INTERNET	34
CHAPTER FOUR NAVIGATING THE MEDIA LANDSCAPE	46
Glossary	58
Source Notes	59
For Further Research	60
Index	62
Image Credits	63
About the Author	64

AT A GLANCE

- Facts are claims that can be confirmed to be true.

- Opinions are claims that cannot be confirmed to be true. They express a person's feelings or personal beliefs.

- Trustworthy news outlets make the difference between facts and opinions clear.

- News organizations employ fact checkers and editors. These workers help keep facts and opinions separate in the organizations' news coverage.

- Today, cable news networks, radio talk shows, and the internet have blurred the line between fact and opinion.

- Anyone can publish information online. They do not need to follow rules of accuracy or fairness.

- Some people create fake news to trick others into supporting their views or believing something that is not true.

- An echo chamber is a space in which a person only encounters information that supports his opinions. Echo chambers reinforce a person's existing beliefs. This can make a person believe that his opinions are facts.

- Reading a variety of sources can help people distinguish fact from opinion. It can help people better understand other points of view.

INTRODUCTION

PODCASTING THE PANDEMIC

On April 23, 2021, entertainer Joe Rogan released a new podcast episode. His show was called *The Joe Rogan Experience*. At the time, it was the world's most popular podcast. Each episode reached about 11 million people.

Rogan covered many topics on his show. He often spoke with experts. They talked about history and science. They discussed sports and even UFOs. The episodes

In 2021, the PolitiFact website asked public health experts to fact-check the COVID-19 claims made in an episode of *The Joe Rogan Experience* podcast. The experts found that the claims were incorrect.

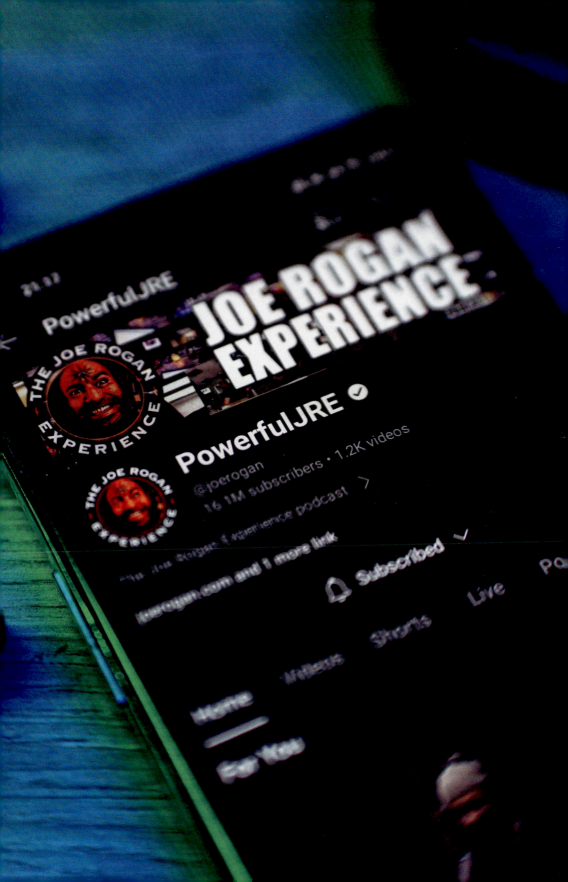

were long. Guests spoke in depth about their knowledge. On the April 23 episode, Rogan spoke with comedian Dave Smith. But Smith and Rogan did not talk about comedy. They talked about the COVID-19 pandemic.

During the COVID-19 pandemic, health organizations such as the Centers for Disease Control and Prevention (CDC) worked to provide accurate information to the public.

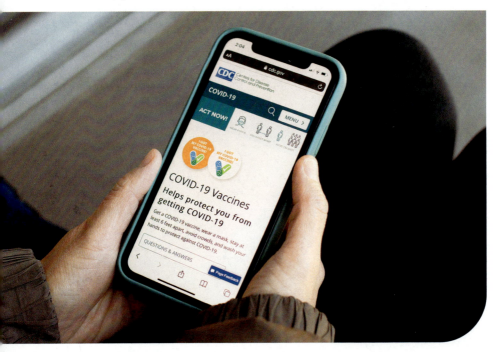

This pandemic had started in March 2020. The dangerous virus had spread around the world. More than 3 million people had died by April 2021. The number of COVID-19 cases had gone up eight weeks in a row. Each day, scientists learned new facts about the virus. Doctors worked to give people accurate information. This way, people could protect themselves.

Rogan and Smith were not doctors or scientists. But they spoke confidently about the virus. Smith said, "If you're a young, healthy person, you really don't have much to worry about with COVID. It's like a scientific fact."[1] Rogan agreed. Later, Rogan made a similar claim. Neither Smith nor Rogan provided sources to back up their statements.

The episode caused a **controversy**. People knew Rogan gave his opinions on his show. But this time, there was no expert to provide the facts. Smith's and Rogan's opinions sounded like facts. Some listeners might believe their claims. This could put their health at risk. Later, Rogan apologized. He said he was not a doctor. He was giving opinions, not facts.

FACT OR OPINION?

It's unclear how Rogan's claims affected his audience's views. But the incident highlighted a problem. In the modern media, the line between fact and opinion has become blurry. With people's health at risk, it is important to understand the difference.

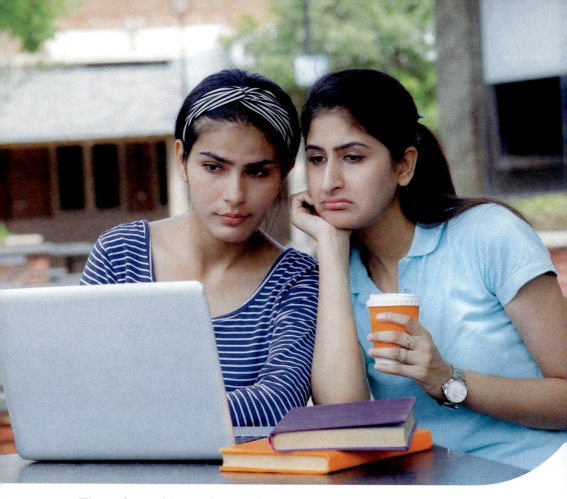

There is a wide variety of information available online. But not all sources are reliable. By using media literacy skills, people can learn how to find factual sources.

Today, people encounter more information than ever before. Facts and opinions are found all over the internet. It can be hard to tell what's true. But people can learn to identify facts and opinions. This is an important part of media literacy.

CHAPTER ONE

WHAT ARE FACTS AND OPINIONS?

A fact is a claim that can be proven true. Facts are clear, direct statements. One example is "In 2023, the French bulldog was the most popular dog breed in the United States." This is a factual statement. It is based on evidence. This evidence can be **confirmed** by others.

An opinion is a claim that cannot be proven true. Opinions are based on a person's feelings or beliefs. An example is

Readers often encounter both facts and opinions in news sources such as the *New York Times* newspaper.

OPEN AT LAST	A.I. LULLABY			ENGINES OF CONNECTION
A MUCH-DELAYED BERLIN AIRPORT	WHEN MACHINES CO-WRITE MUSIC			HALF A CENTURY OF ARTISTIC REINVENTION
PAGE 2 | WORLD	PAGE 3 | TECH			PAGE 14 | CULTURE

The New York Times

INTERNATIONAL EDITION | TUESDAY, NOVEMBER 3, 2020

Four years wasted on a president

Michelle Goldberg

OPINION

It's very hard to catalog all the things we've lost under the presidency of Donald Trump.

As I write this, over 230,000 Americans have lost their lives to Covid-19. Many of our children have lost months of school. Soon, a huge part of the country will lose Thanksgiving.

Because of the Trump administration's barbaric family separation policy, 545 children may be lost to their parents forever. America has lost its status as a leading democracy. We lost Ruth Bader Ginsburg, so we're probably going to lose Roe v. Wade. More people have lost their jobs under Trump than under any president since at least World War II.

Compared with all this, mourning the cultural casualties of the Trump years might be frivolous.

But when I think back, from my obviously privileged position, on the way...

How Trump invaded our brains and destroyed American culture.

Key states are swinging Biden's way, poll shows

Trump could be left with a narrow path to retain the presidency

BY ALEXANDER BURNS AND JONATHAN MARTIN

Joseph R. Biden Jr. holds a clear advantage over President Trump across four of the most important presidential swing states, a new poll shows, but even the support of voters who did not participate in the 2016 election and who now appear to be turning out in large numbers to cast their ballots, models for the Democrats.

Mr. Biden, the former vice president, is ahead of Mr. Trump in the northern battlegrounds of Wisconsin and Pennsylvania, as well as in the Sun Belt states of Florida and Arizona, according to a poll of likely voters conducted by The New York Times and Siena College. His strength is most pronounced in Wisconsin, where he has an outright majority of the vote and leads Mr. Trump by 11 points, 52 percent to 41 percent.

Mr. Biden is leading Donald Trump in four key battleground states just days before the election.

	NYT/Siena Oct. 2020
Ariz. <1 Trump	+6 Biden
Fla. <1 Trump	+3 Biden
Pa. <1 Trump	+6 Biden
	49–43
Wis. <1 Trump	+11 Biden
	52–41

Based on a New York Times/Siena College poll of likely voters from Oct. 26 to Oct. 31

Mr. Biden's performance across the electoral map appears to put him in a stronger position heading into Election Day on Tuesday than any presidential candidate since at least 2008, when in the midst of a global economic crisis Barack Obama captured the White House with 365 Electoral College votes and Mr. Biden at his side.

Mr. Trump's apparent weakness in many of the largest electoral prizes in the United States leaves him with a narrow path to the 270 Electoral College ELECTION, PAGE 4

THEY WON'T BE NONVOTERS THIS TIME Both President Trump and Joseph R. Biden Jr. are benefiting from a surge in voters who didn't vote in 2016. PAGE 6

An oil facility in Cabimas, Venezuela. At stake in President Trump's attempts to overthrow Venezuela's leader were billions of dollars in crude oil, and his re-election prospects.

Trump hits a wall in Venezuela

He had hoped ousting Maduro would help his re-election bid in Florida

BY NICHOLAS CONFESSORE, ANATOLY KURMANAEV AND KENNETH P. VOGEL

When President Trump turned to the Capitol gallery during his State of the Union speech in February to recognize Venezuela's young opposition leader, Juan Guaidó, it seemed like a political masterstroke.

Mr. Guaidó's surprise appearance at the culmination of efforts by foreign policy hawks to shift U.S. strategy in Latin America and dislodge Venezuela's strongman president, Nicolás Maduro — and a thundering ovation from Republicans and Democrats alike. "Mr. Guaidó, please take this message back to your homeland," Mr. Trump proclaimed, to the 38th battleground of South Florida and its enormous population of Cuban-Americans, exiles and others who effectively vanquished Mr. Maduro's survival and, in part, a parable of foreign policy in Mr. Trump's Washington — where ideologues, donors and lobbyists compete to seize the attention of an inexperienced and highly transactional president, warping and reshaping American diplomacy along the way.

The tug of war over Mr. Trump's Venezuela position joined Cuban-American activists and Florida politicians, who his Democratic rival, former Vice President Joseph R. Biden Jr., among Florida's Latino voters, his administration's harsh sanctions have failed to oust Mr. Maduro, while leaving Cuban and Russian transactional president, warping and reshaping American diplomacy along the way.

President Trump had hoped that the opposition leader Juan Guaidó could take over in Venezuela, but popular support for Mr. Guaidó in the country has collapsed.

They included a billionaire donor from Florida, top lobbyists who have earned millions in the influence-business boom of Mr. Trump's first term, and a Venezuelan oligarch, now under federal indictment, who worked to bolster U.S. investments in his country.

At stake was not only the welfare of Venezuelans, but also the flow of billions of dollars in their country's crude oil and, Mr. Trump came to believe, his re-election prospects.

As Mr. Maduro endured, a key architect of Mr. Trump's Venezuela policy left his White House post in September. This summer month, another official met secretly in Mexico with a Maduro ally in a last-ditch effort to persuade Mr. Maduro to step down — which Mr. Trump could have touted as a triumph before November.

A White House spokesman, John Ullyot, said Mr. Trump's leadership had led to broad international pressure on Mr. Maduro. "The president continues to support the Venezuelan people to ensure a future that is democratic and prosperous," he said.

But some former officials who favored a tougher stance on Venezuela VENEZUELA, PAGE 2

A rap star's baptism of fire in Poland's culture wars

LONDON

His focus was on partying. Then a 'vent' on a song cast him into politics.

BY ALEX MARSHALL

Taco Hemingway is a household name in Poland, one of the country's biggest rappers, he has songs that millions have listened to, and before the coronavirus he filled arenas nationwide, where his teenaged fans danced to songs about partying.

But Mr. Hemingway is also a reluctant figurehead in Poland's culture wars, after a song in which he criticized the country's governing right-wing Law and Justice party's threats against L.G.B.T.Q. rights. He has become "wrestled" by the fervent...

WOMEN'S FORUM
FOR THE ECONOMY & SOCIETY

7 KEY ISSUES FOR AN INCLUSIVE RECOVERY

THE VOICE OF GLOBAL LEADERS

"French bulldogs are the cutest." This is an opinion. So is the statement "Pugs should be more popular than French bulldogs." People might agree with these statements. But that does not make them facts. Facts must be backed up with evidence. People need to be able to observe that evidence.

FINDING EVIDENCE

To confirm a fact, people can use the scientific method. Scientists use this process. It involves doing experiments to answer questions. In the 1860s, chemist Louis Pasteur used the scientific method. He wanted to find out why food went bad. Most scientists believed bugs were born from dust and dirt. They said dust and dirt got on food. Then bugs made the food go bad.

Pasteur had a different **theory**. He thought food went bad because of tiny germs. He set up experiments to test his idea. The results supported Pasteur's theory. Other scientists repeated his

Louis Pasteur's experiments with food helped confirm facts about germs. Today, a bust of Pasteur stands in front of the Institut Pasteur in Paris, France.

experiments. They got the same results. Pasteur's idea was confirmed. Germ theory became fact.

Facts aren't limited to science labs. Facts can also be confirmed through observation. A journalist might write about a baseball game. The journalist can give facts about the game. This may include **statistics**, such as the number of home

Fitting in New Facts

As scientists work, they discover new facts. For example, Pluto was once thought to be the ninth planet in the solar system. Then scientists found Pluto-sized objects in an area called the Kuiper Belt. The earlier facts did not change. But with new information, Pluto was viewed differently. It became known as a dwarf planet.

runs. The journalist can talk about the game experience, too. She can write about the smell of hot dogs. She can describe the sound of the crowd. These observations can be confirmed by others at the game. This makes them facts.

TYPES OF SOURCES

When talking about the past, people cannot travel back in time to see events happen. This does not mean historical facts can't be confirmed. People confirm these facts using primary sources. These are descriptions from people who experienced the event firsthand. Journalism is one type of primary source. As reporter John Hersey put it, "Journalism allows its readers to witness history."[2]

To learn about historical events such as Charles Lindbergh's 1927 flight, readers can use primary sources such as newspaper articles from that year.

For example, historians know facts about pilot Charles Lindbergh. They know that on May 21, 1927, Lindbergh finished the first solo flight across the Atlantic Ocean. His plane landed at 10:24 p.m. The flight took 33 hours and 30 minutes. Researchers can confirm this information. They can read Lindbergh's account of the flight. They can look at journalists' reports from New York City. This is where Lindbergh took off. They can read articles from Paris, France. This is where he landed.

Secondary sources also help people learn about events. These sources are made by people who did not witness events firsthand. They bring together facts from primary sources. Secondary sources also provide analysis. This is interpretation of facts. It helps people understand how facts fit together.

Someone studying ancient Egypt might use primary sources. He might read a primary source about King Tutankhamun's tomb. He might learn what archaeologists found inside the tomb. They discovered a mask, jewelry, and an iron knife.

At first, the iron knife might not sound interesting. But secondary sources give more context. Experts believe the knife was made of iron from a meteorite that fell to Earth. With analysis, a fact takes on new meaning.

A COMMON UNDERSTANDING

Facts, analysis, and opinions are helpful when communicating. Facts give people a common understanding. Analysis helps people see how facts connect. It helps them form opinions. When people discuss their opinions with others, they can find new ways of seeing the world.

But sometimes people can't tell the difference between facts and opinions. When this happens, communication

People can find many primary and secondary sources at libraries.

breaks down. It becomes hard to know if something is fact or opinion.

In 2019, University of Illinois Urbana-Champaign researchers did a study. They asked Americans to read twelve statements. They had to identify whether these were facts or opinions. Only 54 percent of people correctly identified six or more statements. These results suggest that Americans need better ways of distinguishing fact from opinion.

CHAPTER TWO

FACTS AND OPINIONS IN TRADITIONAL MEDIA

Distinguishing facts from opinions has not always been difficult. In the past, most people got news from newspapers. Print newspapers have sections. They separate facts and opinions.

Newspapers include labels to guide readers. Some opinion articles are from the newspaper's leadership. These are called editorials. Other opinion articles are from community members. These are op-eds.

Many news organizations offer both print and online content. People can download news apps on their phones. Many have different sections, including opinion, news, and sports.

These usually appear on the page opposite the editorial section. These sections allow newspapers to include multiple viewpoints.

A newspaper writer might interview political candidates. On the editorial page,

Major news organizations, such as the *Washington Post*, have large offices and editorial teams. These teams include editors, writers, creative directors, fact-checkers, and photographers.

the writer might say which candidate he prefers. The op-ed page might do the same for another candidate. Both writers may provide facts to support their opinions. By reading both articles, readers can make more informed decisions.

Newspapers also hire columnists. These writers often know a lot about particular subjects. But they are less focused on giving facts. Instead, they comment on events. They give their own perspectives. Their articles are labeled as commentary.

Columnists often represent common viewpoints. In this way, the newspaper reflects its readers' opinions. Robert Bartley was an opinion editor. He wrote, "Editorial pages deliver the news of ideas, whereas other departments of newspapers deliver the news of events."[3]

CREATING A RECORD

Unlike opinion writers, news journalists try to be **objective**. Their goal is to provide facts about events. They use the Five Ws. This means saying *what* happened and *who* was involved. It also means including *when*, *where*, and *why* an event occurred. By doing this, journalists create a reliable record of the event.

News organizations also hire editors. These workers help confirm journalists' facts. Sometimes, a detail is wrong. The editors correct the detail. They may correct it in the paper's next edition. The correction may appear in the same place where the

Editors work to fact-check sources and verify information in news content such as articles.

error occurred. Other papers have a section for corrections.

Sometimes opinions appear in news articles, too. They come from people involved in an event. Their statements are marked as quotes. Quotes give context about why something occurred. For example, a school board might vote to change school lunches. In an article, a journalist might include a quote explaining the change. She might write, "'Who doesn't want more pizza?' one board member said." The journalist might also include a quote from someone who favored salads. This helps readers get a balanced view of the issue.

BIAS IN THE MEDIA

Like all people, journalists have their own opinions. This is called **bias**. Part of a journalist's job is to keep his biases out of the news. Editors help with this. They review journalists' writing. They help spot bias. This ensures readers get objective accounts.

Traditionally, most TV and radio news organizations have followed these rules. In the 1960s and 1970s, Walter Cronkite hosted *CBS Evening News*. He became known for providing news in an unbiased way. When he delivered opinions, he made it clear. Cronkite famously gave his opinion about the Vietnam War (1954–1975). He said, "We'd like to sum up our findings on Vietnam, an analysis that must be

Many people tune in to the news on radio programs or podcasts. Some people share facts on these shows, but others share opinions.

speculative, personal, **subjective**."[4] Because he was known for being fair, people trusted his opinion.

CHANGING STANDARDS

For years, the US government had rules about how TV and radio organizations provided news. These rules were part of the Fairness Doctrine. An article from the Ronald Reagan Presidential Library

Fair and Balanced?

When Fox News launched, its motto was "Fair and Balanced." This made it sound as if the company was delivering only news. But Fox News was actually giving many opinions. In 2017, the company made a change. Its motto became "Most Watched, Most Trusted."

discusses this. It says, "The Fairness Doctrine mandated broadcast networks devote time to contrasting views on issues of public importance."[5] But in 1987, the government stopped enforcing these rules.

Quickly, news media changed. Radio talk shows became common. Rush Limbaugh became the country's most popular radio host. On his show, Limbaugh did not present a variety of views. Instead, he only gave opinions. These opinions represented his **conservative** political views.

Something similar happened on TV. In 1996, Fox News and MSNBC launched. These cable channels aired 24 hours a day. They needed to fill each hour. They hired journalists, fact-checkers, and editors. But they hired many opinion hosts, too.

Fox News is known for sharing content that has a conservative point of view.

One reason for this change was ratings. Ratings measure how many people watch a show. Some days, there was not much news to report. Ratings went down. Fox News and MSNBC found a solution. They started offering daily content based on opinions. Viewers who shared these opinions would tune in to the content each day.

Fox News became known for its conservative perspective. MSNBC attracted **liberal** viewers. This brought higher ratings to both channels. But it blurred the line between fact and opinion. As a result, people's trust in the news declined. In the 1970s, 70 percent of Americans said that they trusted news media. By 2004, that number had fallen to 44 percent.

CHAPTER THREE

FACTS AND OPINIONS ON THE INTERNET

Today, people can easily access news. On the internet, articles are a click away. People can listen to news coverage at any time. There are also more sources to choose from. People can find content that fits their interests. Someone who moves to another country can read news from his hometown online. People can even watch a rocket launch live from their homes.

People encounter many facts and opinions on social media platforms such as Instagram, X, TikTok, and YouTube.

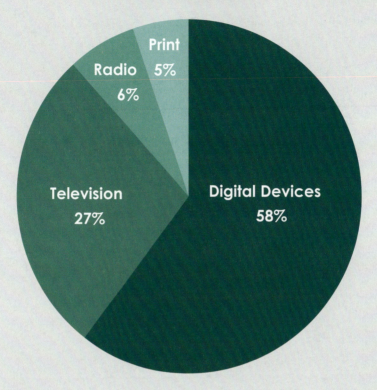

In 2023, a survey asked US adults where they preferred to get their news. Most people said they preferred to get news on digital devices.

Sharing opinions is easier, too. Anyone can share her opinions on social media. Anyone can talk about a topic. A person can start a blog or podcast. She can set up a YouTube channel or Instagram profile.

BENEFITS OF SOCIAL MEDIA

Some changes have brought benefits. Social media connects people with similar interests and experiences. This can make people happier and more confident. One 2023 study found that 58 percent of young people feel more accepted because of social media.

Social media also helps people share ideas. They can discuss changes they want to see in their communities. In 2011, people in Egypt wanted a better government. The country's leader had been in power for 30 years. On social media, Egyptians talked about changes they wanted to see.

They organized protests. After 18 days, the country's leader stepped down. One organizer said, "If you want to liberate a society, all you need is the internet."[6]

DIGITAL DOWNSIDES

The internet has also caused problems. It has blurred the line between fact and opinion. News organizations still separate

Satire

Satire is a type of fake news. But it isn't meant to be taken seriously. It's meant to be funny. The headline "Winter Canceled After 3 Billion Seasons" is satire. If readers are unsure whether something is satire, they should check its source. The website's About page should say the content is satire.

fact and opinion sections. But online, labels can be harder to notice.

There are also more unreliable sources online. Anyone can publish content on the internet. A person can make it look and sound like news. But he doesn't have to follow rules of accuracy and fairness. Some people take advantage of this. They create fake news. This is false or misleading information. But it is presented as news.

Some fake news is meant to influence readers. This is called propaganda. Propaganda presents rumors, opinions, or lies as facts. Its goal is to get people to support a cause or idea. During the COVID-19 pandemic, some people created propaganda. They spread false claims. One was that the US government planned

During the COVID-19 pandemic, many people shared online content about the virus. News organizations worked to provide facts about the health crisis and expose misinformation.

the pandemic. They wanted to persuade people to protest the government's COVID-19 policies.

Some people use fake news to earn money. Companies pay to put ads on websites. When people visit the sites, the website owners earn money. People may use clickbait to get people to visit sites. Clickbait often has over-the-top headlines. A headline might say, "You'll Never Guess What the President Just Did!" Usually, the site linked to the headline doesn't deliver what the headline promises.

Ads can also be presented as news. This is called an advertorial. It may look and sound as if it were written by journalists. It may include quotes and facts. But its goal is to sell a product.

ONLINE AND OFFLINE CONSEQUENCES

Echo chambers are another problem online. An echo chamber is an online space where people with the same ideas gather. When someone shares an opinion, it gets echoed back by people who agree. Some echo chambers are harmless. A person might be a fan of the K-pop group BTS. She might find an online forum with other BTS fans. This gives the person a sense of community.

Other times, echo chambers cause misunderstandings. One example is the flat Earth community. People in this group believe Earth is flat instead of globe shaped. Because others share their opinions, they ignore facts that don't support their beliefs. Echo chambers happen on biased cable news network, too. But on the internet, people have easy access to those who share their opinions.

It's easy to connect with like-minded groups of people on the internet. This can create a sense of community. But sometimes it can prevent people from considering different perspectives.

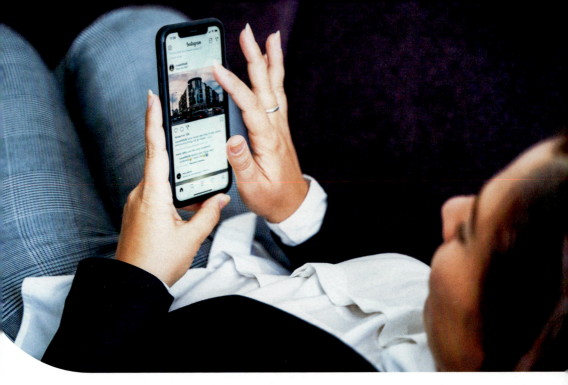

Social media platforms track which posts a user likes or comments on. The platform uses this information to filter similar content into the user's feed.

Social media can cause similar issues. Social media platforms track what users like and don't like. The sites filter content to match each user's interests.

A user might watch many cat videos. In response, the site puts more cat videos in the user's feed. The person might scroll past lizard videos. If this happens, the site will stop showing the user those videos.

This puts the user in what is known as a filter bubble. Social media sites do the same filtering when it comes to delivering facts and opinions.

Over time, echo chambers and filter bubbles can skew people's understandings of facts and opinions. When someone repeatedly sees her own opinions, she might begin to think they are facts. Conversations with people who don't share her opinion can become frustrating. She might stop talking to people who disagree with her. To avoid this problem, people must have a clear understanding of facts and opinions.

CHAPTER FOUR

NAVIGATING THE MEDIA LANDSCAPE

There are many steps people can take to distinguish facts from opinions. When reading online articles, look for labels. An article might be labeled as an editorial, op-ed, or commentary. In ads, people can look for words such as *sponsored*. Laws require ads to be labeled. But sometimes these labels are difficult to spot.

To dig deeper, check who wrote the article. Trustworthy news organizations

At many schools, students learn a variety of media literacy skills. They practice how to distinguish fact from opinion by evaluating sources and fact-checking information.

usually include the author's name. This is called a byline. It gives the author credit for his work. It also gives readers a way to contact someone if the article has an error.

For more information, look at the author's biography, or bio. This gives a

To learn more about a website's goals or practices, readers can check out the site's About page. This can help readers determine whether the site is reliable.

person's background. It can help readers tell if an author is biased. A food scientist writing about the benefits of milk is likely reliable. The same article written by a dairy company employee might not be.

People can also research the website that published the article. Most sites have About pages. These discuss an organization's goals. They inform readers about how the organization confirms facts. The *New York Times* is a popular news source. It has an Editorial Standards page. This page includes a handbook. It lists the rules its journalists follow. It says, "The *Times* treats its readers as fairly and openly as possible. In print and online, we tell our readers the complete . . . truth as best we can learn it."[7] A magazine's About page might be similar. But it might also mention commentary. This can indicate a mix of facts and opinions.

SOCIAL MEDIA AND BEYOND

Today, many people get news through social media. A 2023 study found that about 30 percent of Americans get news from Facebook. Twenty-six percent get news from YouTube. People may come across articles and videos from traditional sources on these sites. They may also find news content created by individuals. With so many sources available, separating fact from opinion can become difficult.

One thing people should consider is the content's tone. Facts are stated in a neutral tone. Opinions often sound emotional.

Many people, especially teens, regularly get their news from social media platforms. TikTok and Instagram are some of the most popular sites.

Many libraries provide resources to help readers evaluate information. Some offer tutorials or checklists that teach people how to distinguish facts from opinions.

The statement "A blue SUV passed by" is factual. The statement "A gas guzzler sped down the road" indicates opinion. Writers express tone in other ways, too. A person might write in capital letters. He may use many exclamation points. This can signal that the person is giving an opinion. His goal is likely to influence readers rather than inform.

Readers should also think about what information a source leaves out. Most issues are complicated. There are facts on each side. Some content may provide facts for only one side. This content is probably leaving out key information. One way people do this is through video editing. Users should be wary of video clips that start and end abruptly. The content creator has likely removed context that doesn't support her opinion.

People should also check if someone is giving reliable facts. To do this, they should check the person's claims. The person might provide links to support his statements. People can use the links to check the sources. A quick way to evaluate a source is to look at its URL. Reliable URLs end in .edu, .gov, .org, or .com. Some fake news sites mimic real news sites. If a site's URL looks strange, it might be fake news.

Deepfakes

Some people create fake videos. These videos replace one person's likeness with another. This allows the creator to make it look like people did or said things they did not. These videos are called deepfakes. Sometimes deepfakes are meant to be funny. But other times, they are meant to upset people.

A HEALTHY MEDIA DIET

Distinguishing facts from opinions is important. It helps people avoid misleading claims. It also helps people make sure they have a healthy media diet. Like a food diet, it's good to have variety. This means taking in a mix of factual news and informed opinions.

A person can test if she is getting too much of one perspective in a source. She can consider whether her views are challenged. Does she come across opinions different from her own? If so, how does she respond? The person may react by dismissing the opinion. This may mean she is in an echo chamber. To fix this, the person can change her media diet. She can seek out reliable sources. She can find sources that express different points of view. Harry S. Truman was the thirty-third US president. He said, "You can never get all the facts from just one newspaper, and unless you have all the facts, you cannot make proper judgments about what is going on."[8]

Engaging with different sources may make a person change his mind. It will help him better understand why people think differently. This can lead to a better understanding of the issue and of other people.

Engaging with a variety of sources can help people develop a healthy media diet.

GLOSSARY

bias
favoring one idea, person, or group above others

confirmed
proven to be true or accurate

conservative
describing a viewpoint that favors established customs

controversy
a dispute or debate involving people with different opinions

liberal
describing a viewpoint that favors social change

objective
not influenced by personal feelings or prejudices

statistics
data or facts in the form of numbers

subjective
influenced or shaped by personal experience or beliefs

theory
a belief or idea about why something happens

SOURCE NOTES

INTRODUCTION: PODCASTING THE PANDEMIC

1. Quoted in Joe Rogan, "#1639—Dave Smith." *The Joe Rogan Experience*, April 23, 2021. http://open.spotify.com.

CHAPTER ONE: WHAT ARE FACTS AND OPINIONS?

2. Quoted in "Nine Inspiring Media Quotes: Journalism, Public Relations and Visual Communication," *Nevada Today*, March 23, 2017. www.unr.edu/nevada-today.

CHAPTER TWO: FACTS AND OPINIONS IN TRADITIONAL MEDIA

3. Quoted in George Melloan, *Free People, Free Markets: How the Wall Street Journal Opinion Pages Shaped America*. New York: Encounter Books, 2017, pp. vii–viii.

4. Quoted in "Final Words: Cronkite's Vietnam Commentary," *NPR*, July 18, 2009. www.npr.org.

5. "Fairness Doctrine," *Ronald Reagan Presidential Library and Museum*, August 9, 2024. www.reaganlibrary.gov.

CHAPTER THREE: FACTS AND OPINIONS ON THE INTERNET

6. Quoted in Lydia Emmanouilidou, "Arab Uprisings: What Role Did Social Media Really Play?" *The World*, December 17, 2020. http://theworld.org.

CHAPTER FOUR: NAVIGATING THE MEDIA LANDSCAPE

7. "Ethical Journalism," *New York Times*, June 20, 2024. www.nytimes.com.

8. Quoted in Flavia Colgan, "The Media Monster That's Eating the Dems," *Philadelphia Inquirer*, February 9, 2009. www.inquirer.com.

FOR FURTHER RESEARCH

BOOKS

A. R. Carser, *What Is Fake News?* San Diego, CA: BrightPoint Press, 2023.

Jacqueline B. Toner, *True or False?: The Science of Perception, Misinformation, and Disinformation.* Washington, DC: Magination Press, 2024.

Marne Ventura, *How to Identify Media Bias.* San Diego, CA: BrightPoint Press, 2025.

INTERNET SOURCES

"The Blur Between Facts and Opinions in the Media," *GCFGlobal*, n.d. http://edu.gcfglobal.org/en.

"How2Internet: Separate Fact from Opinion and Satire Online," *PBS Newshour Classroom*, January 16, 2024. www.pbs.org.

"Interactive Media Bias Chart," *Ad Fontes Media*, 2024. http://adfontesmedia.com.

WEBSITES

Doubt It?
http://doubtit.ca/truth-matters

Doubt It? is a site run by the Canadian Journalism Foundation. It includes tips for evaluating sources, videos from fact-checking experts, a fake news quiz, and other resources.

News Literacy Project
http://newslit.org/for-everyone

The News Literacy Project offers free tools, quizzes, and a podcast to help people sharpen their media literacy skills.

NewseumED
http://newseumed.org

NewseumED offers online resources, videos, historical information, and tools focused on media literacy skills.

INDEX

ads, 40–41, 46
analysis, 19–20, 29

Bartley, Robert, 25
bias, 28–29, 42, 49

clickbait, 41
columnists, 25
COVID-19 pandemic, 8–9, 39–40
Cronkite, Walter, 28–30

deepfakes, 54

echo chambers, 41–42, 45, 55
editorials, 22–25, 46
editors, 25, 26, 28, 31
evidence, 12, 14

fact-checking, 31, 38, 46, 53–54
Fairness Doctrine, 30–31
filter bubbles, 44–45
Fox News, 30, 31–33

Hersey, John, 17

journalists, 16–17, 19, 26, 28, 31, 41, 49

Limbaugh, Rush, 31
Lindbergh, Charles, 18–19

MSNBC, 31–33

newspapers, 22, 24–27, 36, 56

op-eds, 22, 24–25, 46

Pasteur, Louis, 14–16
primary sources, 17–19

radio, 28, 30–31, 36
Rogan, Joe, 6–10

scientific method, 14–16
secondary sources, 19–20
Smith, Dave, 8–10
social media, 36–37, 44–45, 50
statistics, 16–17

television, 28–31, 36
Truman, Harry S., 56

websites, 38, 41, 44–45, 49, 50, 54

IMAGE CREDITS

Cover: © Ground Picture/Shutterstock Images

5: © photobyphotoboy/Shutterstock Images

7: © Rokas Tenys/Shutterstock Images

8: © Tada Images/Shutterstock Images

11: © Deepak Sethi/iStockphoto

13: © Hadrian/Shutterstock Images

15: © HJBC/Shutterstock Images

18: © Library of Congress

21: © Dima Berlin/iStockphoto

23: © DenPhotos/Shutterstock Images

24: © Nicole Glass Photography/Shutterstock Images

27: © antoniodiaz/Shutterstock Images

29: © Nicola Katie/iStockphoto

32: © Leonard Zhukovsky/Shutterstock Images

35: © Tatiana Buzmakova/iStockphoto

36: © Red Line Editorial

40: © FivosVas/Shutterstock Images

43: © Javi Sanz/iStockphoto

44: © DedMityay/Shutterstock Images

47: © Daniel de la Hoz/iStockphoto

48: © T. Schneider/Shutterstock Images

51: © ArtIndividual/iStockphoto

52: © fizkes/Shutterstock Images

57: © Drazen Zigic/Shutterstock Images

ABOUT THE AUTHOR

Kurt Waldendorf is the author of more than a dozen books for young people. When he's not writing or editing, he enjoys indoor rock climbing and running along the shore of Lake Michigan with his dog. He lives in Chicago, Illinois.